SUMMARY OF DELIVER US FROM EVIL

A 40-Day Path Out of Fear, Anxiety, and Depression

KRIS VALLOTTON

DESTINY IMAGE

Destiny Image P.O. Box 310, Shippensburg, PA 17257-0310

This book and all other Destiny Image's books are available at Christian bookstores and distributors worldwide.

For Worldwide Distribution.

Reach us on the Internet: www.destinyimage.com.

ISBN 13 TP: 9798881504328

ISBN 13 eBook: 9798881504335

CONTENTS

INTRODUCTION

In a world teeming with both visible and invisible challenges, the spiritual practice of seeking divine deliverance becomes a vital lifeline for every believer. "Deliver Us from Evil," a chapter inspired by the profound yet simple petition in the Lord's Prayer, explores the essentiality and depth of calling upon God for protection and guidance against evil forces. This prayer, taught by Jesus Himself, encapsulates the spiritual posture that Christians are meant to maintain—constantly aware of and dependent on God's omnipotent care.

The chapter opens with a reflection on the universal need for deliverance, a theme deeply embedded in the fabric of Christian doctrine and daily life. It addresses the theological and practical implications of recognizing our vulnerabilities and the omnipresence of spiritual warfare. By examining scriptural foundations and personal insights, the chapter aims to fortify believers with a robust framework for understanding how prayers for deliverance operate within the broader narrative of God's sovereignty and love.

Deliverance is often perceived as a dramatic escape from peril, yet, as elucidated here, it encompasses much more. It involves ongoing spiritual growth, the practice of steadfast faith, and the cultivation of a life characterized by constant prayer and communion with God. The discussion extends beyond mere theoretical knowledge, proposing actionable insights and reflective exercises that encourage readers to engage actively with the concepts presented.

This introduction sets the stage for a transformative exploration of how living under God's protective promise enables believers to navigate the complexities of life with courage and assurance. It invites readers to rediscover the power embedded in the Lord's Prayer, emphasizing that deliverance is not only about being saved from harm but also about being sustained through everyday trials and triumphs by God's gracious hand.

CHAPTER 1

THE POWER OF NEURAL PATHWAYS

Bible Verse

Romans 12:2 - "Do not be conformed to this world, but be transformed by the renewing of your mind."

Introduction

In this chapter, the author shares a transformative journey through the crisis of a mental and emotional breakdown to understanding the neuroscience behind thought patterns. Drawing from personal experience and scientific insight, the focus is on how the physical structure of our brains can be molded to foster spiritual and mental growth through the concept of neural pathways.

Word of Wisdom

"Renewing our minds means we change not just what we think, but the way we think!" Kris Vallotton

. . .

Main Theme

The main theme of the chapter is the interplay between neuroscience and spiritual practices, particularly how understanding and reshaping our neural pathways can lead to a profound transformation of the mind, aligning more closely with Christ-like thinking and diminishing anxiety and depression.

Key Points

- Thoughts travel on neural pathways, which can be widened by repetition, making certain thinking patterns more prevalent.
- Anxiety and depression can stem from these entrenched neural pathways, leading to a detrimental mental ecosystem.
- Biblical meditation, as practiced by Joshua, is a method for actively constructing new, healthier neural pathways.
- Proactive meditation can shift one's mental landscape from negative loops to empowered, faith-based thinking.
- Continuous practice of meditation and scriptural engagement can fundamentally alter one's mental processes and life outlook.
- The author emphasizes the personal responsibility in renewing one's mind through disciplined spiritual practices.

Key Themes

- **Neural Pathways as Mental Highways:** Just like roads, neural pathways can become broader and more traveled with frequent use. This analogy helps illustrate why certain negative thoughts can become dominant, making it crucial to actively engage in practices that forge new, positive pathways.
- **Impact of Anxiety and Depression:** The author describes these conditions as products of harmful neural pathways, suggesting that mental health issues can be mitigated by altering our brain's pathways, which in turn changes our habitual responses to stress and fear.
- **Scientific and Spiritual Synergy:** By combining neuroscience with biblical principles, the chapter provides a holistic approach to mental health, showing that spiritual practices like meditation are not just doctrinal but have tangible effects on our brain structure.
- **Role of Meditation in Mind Renewal:** Meditation is depicted not as a passive activity but as an active, deliberate practice that can rebuild the brain's pathways, leading to success and fulfillment as seen in the biblical account of Joshua.
- **Transformation Through Discipline:** The commitment to a 40-day journey of meditation and scripture engagement is proposed as a practical way to effect lasting change, emphasizing the role of personal effort in spiritual and mental growth.

Conclusion

The chapter concludes by urging readers to embark on a journey of mind renewal through disciplined scriptural meditation. This practice promises not only a transformation of thought patterns but a profound shift in one's life trajectory, mirroring the biblical promise of prosperity and success through adherence to God's word.

CHAPTER 2

POTTY TRAINING YOUR BRAIN

Bible Verse

Philippians 4:8-9 - "Finally, brothers and sisters, whatever is true, whatever is honorable, whatever is right, whatever is pure, whatever is lovely, whatever is commendable, if there is any excellence and if anything worthy of praise, think about these things."

Introduction

This chapter uses the metaphor of a young woman struggling to control two large dogs to illustrate how unmanaged thoughts can control our lives. The author emphasizes the importance of mastering our thoughts to maintain and enhance our mental and spiritual wellbeing.

Word of Wisdom

"Learning to control our thoughts

instead of allowing our thoughts to control us is probably the single greatest secret to a successful life." Kris Vallotton

Main Theme

The central theme is mastering one's thoughts through intentional mental discipline and the use of scriptural meditation to reinforce positive thinking and mental pathways, leading to a life characterized by peace and success.

Key Points

- Uncontrolled thoughts can dominate and negatively impact our mental health, much like unruly dogs on a leash.
- We must consciously decide what to think about, using our will to guide our mental processes.
- Scriptural meditation can help reshape our thinking patterns toward positivity and peace.
- Verbalizing positive thoughts strengthens them, enhancing their impact on our mental state.
- Regular reflection on uplifting scriptural content is essential for maintaining mental discipline and peace.

Key Themes

- **Mental Discipline as Mastery Over Thoughts:** Just as a dog owner must control their pets, we must take charge of our thoughts. The chapter compares undisciplined thinking to being dragged around by uncontrolled dogs, highlighting the need for assertive mental discipline.
- **Strategic Thought Replacement:** The chapter advises developing a proactive plan for replacing negative thoughts with positive ones. This includes daily affirmations and intentional focus on virtuous and praiseworthy subjects as outlined in Philippians 4:8-9.
- **Reinforcement Through Repetition:** Repeating affirmations and scripture not only cements them in our minds but also builds what the author refers to as mental muscle memory, making positive thinking more automatic over time.
- **Activation of Scriptural Truths:** The practice of writing down and verbalizing truths is encouraged as a method to activate and solidify these truths in our daily lives, promoting a cycle of continual mental renewal and spiritual peace.
- **Monitoring and Managing Thoughts:** Keeping track of one's thought patterns throughout the day is crucial. The author provides practical steps for identifying and countering negative thoughts with scripturally based, positive alternatives.

Conclusion

The chapter concludes with an empowering call to action, urging readers to actively manage their thoughts through disciplined scriptural meditation and affirmations. This approach promises not only a transformation in thinking but an overall enrichment of life, fostering a sense of peace and purpose aligned with divine truths.

CHAPTER 3

SPIRITUAL WARFARE

Bible Verse

Ephesians 6:10-17 - "Finally, be strong in the Lord
and in the strength of His might. Put on the full
armor of God, so that you will be able to stand firm
against the schemes of the devil."

Introduction

The chapter begins with a vivid recounting
of the author's personal struggle with severe anxiety and spiritual oppression,
leading to a profound moment of revelation and
liberation. This personal testimony sets the stage
for a deeper exploration of spiritual warfare, emphasizing the real and present battles believers face
with spiritual forces.

Word of Wisdom

*"Not all of your thoughts are your
own!" Kris Vallotton*

. . .

Main Theme

Spiritual warfare is an integral and unavoidable part of the Christian life, involving battles against demonic forces that seek to oppress and disturb believers. The chapter underscores the necessity of recognizing, confronting, and overcoming these spiritual assaults through God-given strategies and armor.

Key Points

- Christians may not be possessed, but they can be oppressed by demonic forces.
- Recognizing the source of negative thoughts and feelings can be crucial in spiritual warfare.
- Deliverance can come through the power of Jesus' name, bringing immediate relief and peace.
- Wearing the full armor of God as described in Ephesians is essential for protection against spiritual attacks.
- Continuous vigilance and spiritual disciplines are necessary to maintain freedom and peace.

Key Themes

- **Understanding Spiritual Oppression:** The author shares a transformative experience that highlights the distinction between mental illness and spiritual oppression. This theme explores how demonic forces can influence thoughts and feelings, emphasizing the importance of discerning the spiritual origins of our struggles.

- **The Armor of God as Spiritual Protection:** The chapter details each piece of the spiritual armor necessary to withstand demonic attacks, emphasizing that this armor provides not only defense but also the means to proactively combat spiritual threats.
- **Role of Scripture and Prayer in Warfare:** Engaging with Scripture and prayer is portrayed not just as a defensive tactic but as an offensive weapon against spiritual enemies. This practice fortifies the believer's mind and spirit against the lies and attacks of the enemy.
- **Practical Steps to Spiritual Freedom:** Following a dramatic personal story, the author provides actionable steps for readers to claim their spiritual authority and command demonic influences to leave. This includes practical exercises to visualize and apply the armor of God.
- **Maintaining Freedom through Vigilance:** Freedom from spiritual oppression is not a one-time event but requires ongoing diligence and spiritual discipline. The author encourages continuous engagement with Scripture, the Holy Spirit, and the Christian community to sustain freedom and peace.

Conclusion

The chapter concludes by reinforcing the necessity of ongoing vigilance in the life of a believer. By continuously donning the full armor of God and employing biblical truths, believers can not only defend against spiritual assaults but also advance in their spiritual lives, achieving victory and peace in the midst of warfare.

CHAPTER 4

LEARNING TO LEAP

Bible Verse

3 John 2 - "Beloved, I pray that in all respects you may prosper and be in good health, just as your soul prospers."

Introduction

This chapter draws inspiration from the biblical story of Peter healing a lame man at the Temple gate, using it as a metaphor for the interconnectedness of spiritual, physical, and emotional health. The author uses this narrative to highlight the importance of addressing all aspects of our being.

Word of Wisdom

"God often gives us what we need, not what we ask for." Kris Vallotton

Main Theme

The primary theme of this chapter is the holistic approach to health—spirit, soul, and body—as inseparable components that collectively contribute to our overall well-being. The author emphasizes the need for a balanced focus on each aspect to achieve true prosperity and health.

Key Points

- God provides for our needs in ways that surpass our immediate desires or requests.
- True healing and well-being encompass the spirit, soul, and body, not just one aspect.
- The health of our soul is foundational to our overall prosperity and physical health.
- Neglecting the soul can lead to physical and spiritual ailments.
- It's vital to actively care for each dimension of our personhood to live a fulfilled life.

Key Themes

- **The Tridimensional Nature of Personhood:** The author compares our spirit, soul, and body to blended colors that cannot be separated, illustrating how each dimension affects the others. This integration shows that neglect in one area can adversely affect the whole being.
- **The Critical Role of the Soul in Overall Health:** This theme explores the idea that the soul's health directly influences our physical and spiritual health.

The author argues that many physical and spiritual ailments stem from a neglected or unhealthy soul.

- **Biblical Foundation for Holistic Health:** Scriptural references throughout the chapter reinforce the importance of nurturing each aspect of our personhood. The author uses these scriptures to build a theological basis for holistic health practices.

- **Practical Steps to Nurture the Soul:** The chapter provides concrete steps for nurturing the soul, including meditative reading of the scriptures and proactive soul care practices, emphasizing that maintaining soul health is a daily commitment.

- **The Importance of Awareness and Action:** Highlighting the need for awareness of the state of our soul and taking deliberate actions to nurture it, the author encourages readers to engage in self-reflection and to apply biblical principles practically.

Conclusion

The chapter concludes by encouraging readers to not only understand but actively engage in practices that promote a healthy spirit, soul, and body. By taking care of each dimension, believers can experience a more profound sense of wholeness and fulfillment, ultimately leading to a life that truly prospers in all respects as John wishes for his readers in 3 John 2.

CHAPTER 5

LOVE-SICK

Bible Verse

Mark 12:31 - "Jesus said, 'Love your neighbor as yourself.'"

Introduction

This chapter delves into the concept of self-love as a divine requirement, reflecting God's image in ourselves. By using the metaphor of God as the artist and Jesus as the model, the author stresses that negative self-perception is an insult to our Creator and detrimental to our spiritual health.

Word of Wisdom

"Every time we think badly about ourselves, we are insulting the artist and the model." Kris Vallotton

Main Theme

The main theme explores the critical importance of loving oneself as a fundamental aspect of one's identity in Christ. The author argues that understanding and embracing our worth in God's eyes allows us to genuinely love others and accept love in return.

Key Points

- Negative self-perception is often mistaken for humility but is actually harmful.
- True humility involves recognizing and accepting one's value as created in God's image.
- Self-hatred and false humility can lead to depression and other negative emotional states.
- Loving oneself is essential for forming healthy relationships with others.
- Spiritual growth and genuine love for others stem from a healthy self-love.

Key Themes

- **The Destructive Nature of False Humility:** The author challenges the common misunderstanding of humility as self-negation, explaining that it often leads to self-hatred rather than true spiritual humility. This false humility is depicted as a misinterpretation that harms believers' spiritual lives and relationships.

- **Identity and Self-Love in Christ:** Emphasizing that self-love is not egocentric but a recognition of God's creation, the author discusses how a correct understanding of our identity in Christ is necessary for truly loving ourselves and, by extension, loving others effectively.
- **Impacts of Personal History on Self-Perception:** Reflecting on personal experiences with abusive stepfathers, the author illustrates how early life experiences can shape and often distort our self-image, necessitating a reevaluation of our self-worth through the lens of God's truth.
- **Biblical Foundations for Self-Worth:** The use of Scripture to build a case for self-worth underpins the theological argument that loving oneself is inherently biblical and essential for a healthy Christian life.
- **Practical Steps to Embrace Self-Love:** The chapter provides practical exercises for the reader to engage with, such as writing down things they love about themselves and meditating on specific Scriptures that affirm God's love and design for them.

Conclusion

The chapter concludes by affirming that loving oneself is not an act of selfishness but a reflection of understanding God's love. By accepting and valuing ourselves as God's beloved creations, we unlock the ability to love and be loved according to the fullness of the life Christ intends for us. This realization is portrayed as both liberating and essential for holistic spiritual living.

CHAPTER 6

LOVE LOOKS LIKE SOMETHING

Bible Verse

Luke 10:28 - "Do this and you will live."

Introduction

This chapter uses the story of the Good Samaritan to illustrate the practical and actionable nature of love, as taught by Jesus. The narrative is presented to challenge the traditional notions of love as a mere feeling, promoting it instead as a deliberate and tangible expression of care and compassion towards others and oneself.

Word of Wisdom

"Love isn't a feeling! Love is inconvenient, compassionate, caring, and kind."
Kris Vallotton

Main Theme

The main theme focuses on the actionable nature of love, emphasizing that true love involves taking concrete steps to care for others, even when it is inconvenient or challenging. It also explores the importance of self-compassion and treating oneself as a valued neighbor.

Key Points

- Love requires action and is demonstrated through compassionate deeds.
- Self-love is crucial for effectively loving others.
- Loving actions often involve personal sacrifice and stepping into uncomfortable situations.
- We should treat ourselves with the same compassion we are called to offer others.
- Reflecting on and caring for our own soul is essential for holistic well-being.

Key Themes

- **Concrete Expressions of Love:** The Samaritan's actions exemplify love as a series of deliberate acts aimed at alleviating suffering and providing for needs. This portrayal challenges readers to reconsider their own actions towards others as measures of their love.
- **Self-Love as a Foundation for Other-Love:** Just as the Samaritan cared for a

stranger, the author urges readers to apply the same level of care to themselves. Recognizing one's own needs and addressing them compassionately is presented as a prerequisite to genuinely loving others.

- **Interconnection of Love and Sacrifice:** True love often requires personal sacrifice—this theme is explored through the Samaritan who not only helped the wounded man but also paid for his continued care, illustrating that love sometimes demands more than the minimum effort.
- **Reflection and Care of One's Soul:** Like King David, who nurtured a friendship with his soul, the author encourages readers to engage in introspective practices to better understand and care for their inner selves.
- **Practical Application of Love:** The chapter concludes with practical advice on how to engage with and improve one's internal state, suggesting that caring for one's soul is an ongoing process that enhances one's ability to love others effectively.

Conclusion

The chapter wraps up by reinforcing that love, both towards oneself and others, should manifest in visible and practical ways. By encouraging readers to actively engage with their souls and to express love through actions, the author aims to inspire a more profound and active commitment to living out the biblical command to love our neighbors as ourselves.

CHAPTER 7

THE SHAME GAME

Bible Verse

1 John 1:5-9 - "If we walk in the Light as He Himself is in the Light, we have fellowship with one another, and the blood of Jesus His Son cleanses us from all sin."

Introduction

This chapter explores the destructive impact of shame on personal connections and spiritual life, drawing insights from Dr. Brené Brown's research on vulnerability and shame. It connects these concepts with biblical teachings on confession, forgiveness, and authentic living.

Word of Wisdom

"Shame is the fear of disconnection; it's vulnerability that breaks the power of shame." Kris Vallotton

. . .

Main Theme

The main theme focuses on overcoming shame through vulnerability and authenticity, supported by a biblical framework that encourages confession and walking in the light as pathways to spiritual cleansing and deeper community connections.

Key Points

- Shame disrupts our ability to connect with others and with God.
- Vulnerability is the antidote to shame, fostering connection and healing.
- Authenticity involves being true to oneself and rejecting false identities.
- Courage and compassion are essential for embracing vulnerability.
- Walking in spiritual light involves honest self-reflection and confession.

Key Themes

- **Connection as a Fundamental Human Need:** Dr. Brené Brown's research underscores that connection is essential for psychological and emotional well-being. This chapter aligns her findings with the Christian view that we are created for fellowship with God and others, suggesting that disconnection, fueled by shame, is profoundly damaging.

- **Vulnerability as a Gateway to Healing:** Vulnerability is presented as both challenging and healing, enabling individuals to overcome shame and build genuine relationships. The courage to be vulnerable is linked to a sense of worthiness and belonging, which are foundational to Christian fellowship.
- **The Role of Authenticity in Spiritual Life:** Authenticity is crucial for overcoming shame and living out one's true identity in Christ. The chapter encourages letting go of who we think we should be to embrace who we are, which is essential for genuine spiritual and personal growth.
- **Biblical Perspective on Confession and Forgiveness:** The scriptural meditation emphasizes that confession is a powerful act of vulnerability that leads to forgiveness and cleansing. This process not only addresses the symptoms of shame but also its spiritual root causes.
- **Practical Steps Towards Authentic Living:** The chapter provides practical advice on engaging with one's inner self through meditation, confession, and embracing one's true identity in Christ. These steps are aimed at fostering a lifestyle that rejects shame and embraces the healing light of God's truth.

Conclusion

The chapter concludes by advocating for a life of openness and authenticity, where believers are encouraged to step out of the shadows of shame and into the light of God's truth. By doing so, they can experience the fullness of life intended by God, marked by deep connections with others and a clear conscience before God. This transformation is achieved through the power of vulnerability, courage, and living true to one's identity in Christ.

CHAPTER 8

SCARRED FOR LIFE

Bible Verse

Romans 8:1-2 - "Therefore there is now no condemnation for those who are in Christ Jesus. For the law of the Spirit of life in Christ Jesus has set you free from the law of sin and of death."

Introduction

This chapter reflects on the transformative power of Christ's resurrection, highlighting how Jesus's scars from crucifixion became symbols of hope and redemption. It draws a parallel to our own lives, suggesting that our scars, whether physical or emotional, can similarly testify to God's grace and healing.

Word of Wisdom

"It's often our scars that communicate our redemption story." Kris Vallotton

Main Theme

The main theme centers around the concept that our past wounds and scars are not marks of shame but are testimonies to God's grace and Christ's redemptive power. These scars should be viewed as symbols of victory over past pains and challenges, reflecting our growth and God's faithfulness.

Key Points

- Jesus's resurrection appearance included showing His scars as proof of His victory and identity.
- Our scars can be viewed as evidence of survival and sources of empowerment.
- Hiding our scars out of shame can prevent others from seeing God's work in our lives.
- Sharing our scar stories can encourage and comfort others who are struggling.
- Living authentically involves acknowledging our past and the growth that comes from it.

Key Themes

- **Transformation Through Vulnerability:** By embracing vulnerability, as Jesus did, we can transform our scars into powerful testimonies of divine grace. The chapter emphasizes that showing our scars can help dismantle the walls of fear and isolation we often build around ourselves.
- **No Condemnation in Christ:** The assurance that we are free from

condemnation in Christ encourages us to live openly and authentically. This freedom should empower us to share our past with courage, knowing that our identity is secured in God's forgiveness and not in our imperfections.

- **Scars as Symbols of Divine Grace:** Just as Christ's scars were visible and recognized by His disciples as marks of His love and sacrifice, our scars, too, can be seen as markers of God's intervention and care in our lives. They are not just reminders of past pain but also of survival and resilience.
- **Peer Pressure vs. Authentic Living:** The societal pressure to appear perfect is challenged by the biblical call to bear one another's burdens. Authenticity in sharing our struggles and victories fosters deeper community and spiritual connections.
- **Empowering Others Through Personal Stories:** Sharing the stories behind our scars can act as a catalyst for healing, not just for ourselves but also for others. It provides a platform for deeper connections and mutual support within the community.

Conclusion

The chapter concludes by encouraging readers to view their scars not as blemishes but as badges of honor that illustrate the story of their journey with Christ. It calls for a shift from shame to celebration, promoting a life of transparency and authenticity that allows others to find hope and strength in our testimonies of God's redeeming love.

CHAPTER 9

NOBODY LOVES ME

Bible Verse

Ephesians 1:3-8 - "He chose us in Him before the foundation of the world, that we would be holy and blameless before Him. In love He predestined us to adoption as sons and daughters through Jesus Christ to Himself, according to the good pleasure of His will."

Introduction

This chapter explores how our self-perception and the respect we accord ourselves directly influence how others treat us. It emphasizes the importance of recognizing our inherent value as God's creation to foster healthier relationships and better treatment from others.

Word of Wisdom

"We teach people how to treat us by the way we treat ourselves." Kris Vallotton

. . .

Main Theme

The central theme of the chapter is that self-respect and self-love are crucial in setting the standard for how others perceive and treat us. It argues that by valuing ourselves as God values us, we can improve our interactions and relationships.

Key Points

- Our treatment of ourselves sets expectations for how others should treat us.
- Loving ourselves is crucial for allowing others to love us.
- Self-neglect can lead to a cycle of rejection and negative self-perception.
- Our identity in Christ should be the foundation of our self-esteem.
- Demonstrating self-respect can change how others perceive and interact with us.

Key Themes

- **Influence of Self-Perception on External Treatment:** The way we care for ourselves and present ourselves to the world has a significant impact on how others treat us. If we value and respect ourselves, it teaches others to treat us with the same respect.
- **Breaking the Cycle of Rejection Through Self-Respect:** By treating

ourselves with the dignity and respect we deserve as creations made in the image of God, we can break the cycle of rejection. This self-respect not only improves our self-esteem but also makes us more attractive to others in a positive way.

- **The Role of Identity in Christ in Shaping Self-Perception:** Understanding our identity as chosen and loved by God before the foundation of the world empowers us to view ourselves with honor and worth, which is essential for healthy self-regard and interpersonal relations.
- **Practical Steps to Enhance Self-Worth:** The chapter provides actionable advice on improving self-perception through spiritual affirmations and recognizing our royal roots in Christ. These practices encourage us to maintain a posture of self-respect and demand it from others.
- **Transformation Through Generosity and Identity Recognition:** The personal anecdote about the YMCA basketball team illustrates how acts of generosity and recognition of our true identity in Christ can transform how others treat us, fostering a new cycle of positive interactions and mutual respect.

Conclusion

The chapter concludes by urging readers to live out their identity in Christ actively and to treat themselves with the respect and love they deserve. By doing so, they set a standard for others to follow, leading to healthier and more fulfilling relationships. This change begins with internal transformation and extends outward, influencing every aspect of our interactions and how we are perceived by others.

CHAPTER 10

MAKING DEALS WITH THE DEVIL

Bible Verse

Ephesians 4:25-27 - "Therefore, ridding yourselves of falsehood, SPEAK TRUTH EACH ONE OF YOU WITH HIS NEIGHBOR, because we are parts of one another. BE ANGRY, AND YET DO NOT SIN; do not let the sun go down on your anger, and do not give the devil an opportunity."

Introduction

This chapter delves into the spiritual discernment of demonic influences in our lives and how Christians can inadvertently open doors to these forces through negative confessions or actions. It highlights a real-life example from a church setting where spiritual discernment identified and addressed a spirit of suicide.

Word of Wisdom

"What do I do now? Ask Jesus to

forgive you, and then renounce the spirit of death." Kris Vallotton

Main Theme

The main theme is the critical importance of vigilance over one's spiritual doors, ensuring they remain closed to demonic influences. The chapter emphasizes the power of repentance and renunciation in overcoming these spiritual battles.

Key Points

- Spiritual discernment can reveal hidden demonic influences affecting individuals.
- Negative statements or emotional pain can open doors to demonic attacks.
- Repentance and renunciation are powerful tools for closing these doors.
- God provides ways to escape and endure temptations and spiritual attacks.
- Maintaining spiritual hygiene requires constant vigilance and truthfulness.

Key Themes

- **Connection Between Emotional States and Spiritual Vulnerability:** The example of a woman battling suicidal thoughts illustrates how personal crises can lead to spiritual vulnerabilities. This theme explores how emotions like despair can open individuals to attacks if not handled with spiritual awareness and intervention.

- **Role of Spiritual Discernment in Community Healing:** The church leader's use of spiritual discernment serves as a model for pastoral care, demonstrating how spiritual gifts can identify and address hidden battles within the church community. This proactive approach is vital for fostering a healing and supportive environment.

- **Importance of Guarding One's Spiritual Doors:** This theme emphasizes the necessity of being aware of what we mentally and verbally agree with. It discusses how seemingly innocuous decisions or statements can grant demonic spirits access to our lives, thus the need for constant vigilance.

- **The Power of Repentance and Renunciation:** Through repentance and the renouncing of specific agreements with darkness, Christians can reclaim their spiritual authority. This process is highlighted as both a personal and communal practice that reinforces one's identity in Christ and alignment with His truth.

- **Practical Steps for Spiritual Maintenance:** The chapter outlines practical measures for maintaining spiritual health, such as regular self-examination, confession, and the application of Scripture to daily life. These steps help believers fortify their defenses against spiritual attacks and live in freedom.

Conclusion

The chapter concludes with a call to action for readers to actively engage in spiritual self-care by identifying and renouncing any unholy agreements they may have made, knowingly or unknowingly. By embracing the truths of Scripture and relying on the Holy Spirit for guidance, believers can live in victory over demonic influences and grow in their spiritual walk.

CHAPTER 11

GRASSHOPPERS OR GHOSTBUSTERS

Bible Verse

Romans 8:31-39 - "What then shall we say to these things? If God is for us, who can be against us?"

Introduction

This chapter challenges the reader to confront and overcome the spirit of inadequacy. By recounting the story of the Israelite spies who felt like grasshoppers before the giants in the Promised Land, the chapter illustrates how a distorted self-perception can sabotage God's promises for us.

Word of Wisdom

"The dogs of doom stand at the doors of our destiny." Kris Vallotton

Main Theme

The main theme of the chapter is overcoming feelings of inadequacy and fear by embracing the truth of God's word. It stresses the importance of recognizing and resisting the lies that make us feel insufficient and unworthy of the promises God has for our lives.

Key Points

- The perception of inadequacy is often a distortion not based on reality.
- Fear and inadequacy prevent us from claiming what God has promised us.
- Truth is a powerful weapon against the lies of inadequacy.
- God's perspective is that we are more than conquerors through Him.
- Embracing our identity in Christ allows us to overcome fears and take bold actions.

Key Themes

- **Distorted Self-Perception as a Barrier to Success:** The story of the spies illustrates how a distorted perception of ourselves, viewed through the lens of fear, can prevent us from stepping into our God-given destinies. This theme emphasizes that our self-view must align with God's view to overcome these giants.
- **Biblical Strategy for Conquering Fear:** The chapter outlines a biblical strategy for dealing with feelings of

inadequacy, using the example of David and Goliath to show that what seems like an insurmountable obstacle can actually be an opportunity for God to demonstrate His power through us.

- **The Role of Spiritual Discernment in Recognizing Lies:** Spiritual discernment is highlighted as a key tool for distinguishing between the voices of fear and the voice of wisdom. This discernment is essential for navigating challenges and stepping into new opportunities with confidence.

- **Practical Steps to Reaffirming One's Identity in Christ:** The chapter provides practical advice on how to daily reaffirm one's identity in Christ through scriptural meditation and truth infusion, which help fortify believers against the lies of inadequacy.

- **Empowerment Through God's Promises:** By focusing on the promises of Romans 8:31-39, the theme explores how embracing these truths empowers believers to act boldly and confidently, regardless of how intimidating the challenges may appear.

Conclusion

The chapter concludes with a call to action for believers to view themselves as conquerors through Christ. It encourages readers to reject the lies of fear and inadequacy by holding onto the truth of their divine heritage and the overwhelming victory available through Jesus. This shift in perspective is essential for living out the fullness of life that God intends for each believer.

CHAPTER 12

SUICIDE SOLUTION

Bible Verse

Psalm 23:4 - "Even though I walk through the valley of the shadow of death, I fear no evil, for You are with me; Your rod and Your staff, they comfort me."

Introduction

This chapter explores the spiritual dimensions of suicidal thoughts, identifying them as manifestations of a demonic spirit aimed at ending lives and derailing destinies. It draws from biblical examples and personal anecdotes to highlight the pervasive and deceptive nature of this spirit.

Word of Wisdom

"Where there's a shadow, there has to be light! In our distress, Jesus is nearer to us than we might think." Kris Vallotton

Main Theme

The central theme is the battle against the spirit of suicide through spiritual awareness, divine truth, and the power of God's presence. It emphasizes the importance of recognizing our value in God's plan and the deceptive tactics of the enemy that lead to despair.

Key Points

- Suicide is often influenced by demonic forces seeking to destroy lives.
- Personal despair can open doors to suicidal temptations.
- God's presence and truth provide the strength to overcome these dark thoughts.
- Sharing struggles with trusted individuals can diminish the power of these temptations.
- Reaffirming one's identity in Christ is crucial for resisting and overcoming suicidal thoughts.

Key Themes

- **The Role of Spiritual Warfare in Combating Suicide:** This theme delves into the concept that suicidal thoughts can be a form of spiritual attack, emphasizing the need for spiritual discernment and intervention. It suggests that understanding the spiritual basis of these thoughts is key to effectively countering them.

- **Empowerment Through Scriptural Truths:** The chapter underscores the importance of grounding oneself in biblical truths to combat the lies of inadequacy and despair that feed suicidal thoughts. It illustrates how scriptures can be a source of strength and a tool for mental and spiritual renewal.
- **The Importance of Community in Facing Life's Valleys:** Highlighting the necessity of not facing struggles alone, this theme advocates for openness and vulnerability within a supportive community as a means of dispelling the isolation that often accompanies suicidal thoughts.
- **Overcoming Through God's Promises and Presence:** Reflecting on God's promises and His constant presence provides reassurance during times of mental and spiritual crisis. This theme encourages believers to lean on God's unchanging character and His ability to sustain them through all challenges.
- **Practical Steps for Maintaining Spiritual and Mental Health:** Offering practical advice for daily spiritual upkeep, such as meditating on God's word, engaging in prayer, and proclaiming biblical truths, this theme is geared towards building resilience against the spiritual roots of depression and suicidal thoughts.

Conclusion

The chapter concludes by reaffirming the power of God's love and the efficacy of His word against the backdrop of spiritual warfare. It calls for vigilance, continuous spiritual maintenance, and the embrace of community support to safeguard against the lies that precipitate suicidal thoughts. By anchoring ourselves in the truth of our divine purpose and identity, we can overcome the darkest valleys and emerge stronger and more connected to our faith and community.

CHAPTER 13

ALL ABOARD THE PEACE TRAIN

Bible Verse

Philippians 4:6-9 - "Do not be anxious about anything, but in everything by prayer and pleading with thanksgiving let your requests be made known to God. And the peace of God, which surpasses all comprehension, will guard your hearts and minds in Christ Jesus."

Introduction

This chapter discusses the importance of actively maintaining peace in our lives by managing how we react to stress and anxiety. Through the story of an instructor named Jane, it illustrates a proactive approach to reclaiming peace by identifying and addressing disruptions as they occur.

Word of Wisdom

"I want us to steward our peace! This

is a proactive, powerful lifestyle rooted in the leadership of the Holy Spirit and empowered by the grace of the Lord Jesus."
Kris Vallotton

Main Theme

Focusing on the stewardship of peace rather than merely managing stress, the chapter emphasizes the need to actively maintain a state of peace by being mindful of what affects our emotional and spiritual wellbeing.

Key Points

- Peace can be actively managed and maintained like a financial account.
- Identifying the exact moment of losing peace can help in addressing the root cause.
- Emotional disruptions can often be traced back to specific events or interactions.
- Proactively dealing with these disruptions restores peace and prevents stress accumulation.
- The scripture Philippians 4:6-9 offers a biblical foundation for finding peace through prayer and focus on positive thoughts.

Key Themes

- **Proactive Peace Management versus Reactive Stress Management:** The idea of keeping short accounts with peace, as introduced by Jane, is contrasted with the common approach of stress management. This theme explores how a proactive approach to peace through self-awareness and immediate action can prevent the build-up of stress and anxiety.

- **The Impact of Emotional Disruptions on Peace:** Detailed exploration of how specific interactions, such as receiving upsetting news, can disrupt peace, and how recognizing these triggers can empower individuals to regain control over their emotional state. It underscores the importance of addressing these issues promptly to maintain inner peace.

- **Spiritual and Practical Tools for Peace Stewardship:** Discusses the spiritual practices such as prayer, meditation on Scriptures, and practical strategies like making lists and planning as means to steward peace. This theme advocates for a holistic approach, combining spiritual strength with practical actions to manage one's peace.

- **Transformative Power of Maintaining Peace:** By maintaining peace, individuals can transform their internal landscape, which in turn improves their interactions with others and overall quality of life. This theme encourages readers to consider the broader impact of their internal peace on their external circumstances.

- **Role of Thanksgiving and Positive Reflection in Peace Stewardship:** The practice of recording and reflecting on things one is thankful for is highlighted as a powerful tool in reinforcing a peaceful mindset and combating the onslaught of negative emotions.

Conclusion

The chapter concludes by urging readers to adopt Jane's method of keeping short accounts with peace by being vigilant about their emotional state and taking immediate action to address disturbances. It promotes a lifestyle of peace stewardship, rooted in biblical principles and supported by practical actions, as essential for a fulfilling and spiritually healthy life.

CHAPTER 14

LIVING FUTURE-PRESENT

Bible Verse

Philippians 3:13-14 - "Brothers and sisters, I do not regard myself as having taken hold of it yet; but one thing I do: forgetting what lies behind and reaching forward to what lies ahead, I press on toward the goal for the prize of the upward call of God in Christ Jesus."

Introduction

This chapter explores the transformative power of living a life focused on future possibilities rather than past regrets. Through biblical examples and personal insights, it encourages readers to embrace a forward-thinking mindset that aligns with God's perspective.

Word of Wisdom

"Love rewrites our history! God doesn't just forgive us; His redemption rewrites our history...He retells our story

from a loving Father's perspective!" Kris Vallotton

Main Theme

The main theme centers on overcoming the paralysis of past regrets by focusing on future potentials and God's promises. It underscores the necessity of releasing past failures to fully engage with God's plans for our lives.

Key Points

- Regret can cripple potential by keeping individuals focused on past failures.
- Sarah's biblical story illustrates how God reinterprets our past with a narrative of faith and fulfillment.
- Living "future-present" means aligning current actions with future prophetic realities.
- Paul's example of pressing forward despite his past highlights the power of a future-focused life.
- God's perspective on our past is redefined through His love and forgiveness.

Key Themes

- **The Destructive Nature of Regret and the Healing Power of Future Focus:** The detrimental impact of dwelling on past mistakes is contrasted with the liberating effect of focusing on future promises. This theme elaborates on how regret ties one's emotions to unchangeable past events, while a future-present outlook aligns one's actions with God's ongoing redemptive work.

- **Biblical Examples of Redemption and Future Promise:** By examining the lives of Sarah and Paul, the narrative discusses how biblical figures overcame their past by embracing God's promises for their future. This theme encourages readers to view their own lives through the lens of divine possibility rather than human failure.

- **Practical Strategies for Shifting Focus from Past to Future:** This theme offers practical advice on how to shift one's focus from past regrets to future goals, including meditation on scriptures and active re-framing of past experiences in light of God's word.

- **The Role of Faith in Overcoming Regrets:** Faith is presented as a crucial element in moving past regrets. This theme explores how faith in God's goodness and His plans can transform how we view our past and energize our present actions.

- **Emotional and Spiritual Benefits of Living Future-Present:** The benefits of living a life oriented towards future promises, such as increased peace, joy, and fulfillment, are detailed. This theme emphasizes how a future-present mindset facilitates deeper spiritual growth and personal development.

Conclusion

The chapter concludes by affirming that living future-present is not just an optimistic outlook but a biblically mandated and spiritually fruitful lifestyle. It calls readers to actively reject the paralysis of regret by embracing the dynamic journey toward fulfilling God's prophetic purposes for their lives. This proactive stance redefines one's identity and destiny through the lens of divine love and eternal purpose.

CHAPTER 15

THE POWER OF LAUGHTER

Bible Verse

Proverbs 17:22 - "A joyful heart is good medicine, but a broken spirit dries up the bones."

Introduction

This chapter explores the profound impact of laughter on mental and physical health, drawing from scientific studies and personal anecdotes to illustrate how laughter can transform painful experiences into moments of relief and joy.

Word of Wisdom

"If joy is a medicine, I want to be a pharmacist!" Kris Vallotton

Main Theme

Laughter not only provides temporary relief from pain but also has long-term healing effects on our emotional and physical well-being, proving to be a vital tool in overcoming life's challenges.

Key Points

- Norman Cousins' experience with laughter therapy showcases its effectiveness in managing pain and fostering recovery.
- Laughter can act as a natural anesthetic, providing significant relief from physical discomfort.
- Incorporating laughter into daily life can combat depression and anxiety.
- It is essential to actively seek moments of humor to cultivate a joyful heart.
- Reflecting on instances of laughter can help maintain emotional health.

Key Themes

- **Scientific Validation of Laughter's Benefits:** Modern science supports the therapeutic benefits of laughter, validating age-old wisdom about its healing properties. Studies indicate that laughter can reduce pain, lower stress, and boost immune function, making it a powerful ally in health management.
- **Laughter as a Catalyst for Emotional Recovery:** Laughter serves as a crucial

coping mechanism during times of stress, anxiety, or sadness. By shifting focus from distress to joy, laughter facilitates emotional resilience and can dramatically alter our perception of challenging situations.

- **Strategic Application of Laughter Therapy:** Implementing laughter intentionally as part of therapy can accelerate recovery from emotional and physical ailments. This proactive approach can transform how individuals deal with pain and adversity.

- **Historical and Personal Perspectives on Laughter:** Drawing from personal stories and historical examples, laughter is shown to transcend cultural and temporal boundaries, offering universal benefits. These narratives highlight laughter's role in overcoming adversity and fostering human connection.

- **Cultivating a Lifestyle of Joy and Laughter:** Building habits that incorporate laughter into daily routines can ensure sustained benefits. This includes engaging with humorous media, sharing jokes, or simply reminiscing about funny moments, all of which fortify emotional health.

Conclusion

The chapter concludes with a call to action for readers to embrace laughter not just as a reaction to humor, but as a deliberate practice to enhance life quality and health. It emphasizes that laughter is more than just a temporary diversion; it is a vital component of a healthy, joyful life, capable of rewriting painful narratives into stories of triumph and resilience.

CHAPTER 16

FORGIVENESS RESTORES THE STANDARD

Bible Verse

Colossians 3:12-13 - "So, as those who have been chosen of God, holy and beloved, put on a heart of compassion, kindness, humility, gentleness, and patience; bearing with one another, and forgiving each other, whoever has a complaint against anyone; just as the Lord forgave you, so must you do also."

Introduction

This chapter delves into the transformative power of forgiveness, illustrating through personal anecdotes and biblical teachings how forgiving ourselves and others restores life's ethical standards and promotes emotional healing.

Word of Wisdom

"Forgiveness restores the standard... it erases my infraction and wipes my slate clean." Kris Vallotton

. . .

Main Theme

Forgiveness is not merely an emotional release but a restoration of moral and spiritual order, which aligns our actions with divine principles and enhances our interpersonal relationships.

Key Points

- Forgiveness involves acknowledging wrongs and sincerely apologizing to those affected.
- It sets a standard for behavior and underscores the non-repetitive nature of forgiveness.
- Children learn standards of respect and treatment of others through observing parental behavior.
- Immediate family members are often the first to experience the effects of our behavior and need for forgiveness.
- Forgiveness is both a personal release and a communal restoration.

Key Themes

- **The Educational Role of Forgiveness:** Forgiveness teaches ethical behavior by example, as shown when a parent apologizes to a child for misbehavior, setting a precedent for respecting others and taking responsibility.

- **Forgiveness as a Reset Mechanism:** When we forgive or are forgiven, it acts like a reset button, not only clearing our conscience but also restoring broken relationships to their original state of respect and understanding.
- **Impact of Forgiveness on Youth:** Young people, especially children, are impressionable and take cues from how their elders handle conflict and resolution. Discussing forgiveness openly with them can profoundly impact their development and understanding of relationships.
- **Long-term Benefits of Forgiveness:** Engaging in forgiveness can lead to healthier relationships and a more fulfilling life, as grudges and resentments are replaced with peace and compassion.
- **Forgiveness and Spiritual Health:** From a spiritual perspective, forgiveness aligns us with the divine attribute of mercy, facilitating deeper spiritual growth and connection with the divine.

Conclusion

The chapter concludes by reinforcing the notion that forgiveness is crucial for personal peace and community harmony. It calls readers to practice forgiveness actively, not just as a response to wrongs but as a standard approach to living a fulfilled and spiritually aligned life.

CHAPTER 17

FEAR IS FAITH IN THE WRONG KINGDOM

Bible Verse

Nehemiah 6:10-13 - "When I entered the house of Shemaiah...he said, 'Let's meet together in the house of God, within the temple, and let's close the doors of the temple, for they are coming to kill you, and they are coming to kill you at night.' But I said, 'Should a man like me flee? And who is there like me who would go into the temple to save his own life? I will not go in.'"

Introduction

This chapter explores the concept of fear as misplaced faith and emphasizes the importance of aligning our beliefs with God's truth rather than our anxieties or the deceptive whispers of adversaries.

Word of Wisdom

"Fear is actually faith in the wrong kingdom!" Kris Vallotton

Main Theme

Understanding fear as a form of faith highlights the necessity of choosing to trust in God's kingdom over succumbing to the anxieties that can dominate our earthly experience.

Key Points

- Fear often stems from negative stories we tell ourselves rather than reality.
- Identifying the root of fears can diminish their power over us.
- Fear distorts our perception, while faith in God restores clarity.
- Historical figures like Nehemiah exemplify overcoming fear through divine trust.
- Fear can hinder our mission, but faith propels us toward divine fulfillment.

Key Themes

- **The Paralyzing Effect of Fear:** Fear, when viewed as misplaced faith, can paralyze our ability to act according to God's will. Recognizing fear as a faith in negative outcomes empowers us to realign with faith in God's plans.

- **Historical and Biblical Insight on Fear:** Nehemiah's refusal to succumb to fear, despite significant threats, illustrates the profound impact of steadfast faith in overcoming challenges and completing God's work.
- **Personal Responsibility in Managing Fear:** Actively choosing faith over fear involves recognizing moments when fear distorts reality and deliberately refocusing on truths that align with God's word.
- **The Role of Community in Confronting Fear:** Sharing our fears within a supportive community can diminish their power and reinforce a collective strength grounded in faith.
- **Transformative Power of Faith:** Faith has the capacity to transform not only individual moments of fear but also to redefine life's trajectory by focusing on divine truth over earthly anxiety.

Conclusion

The chapter concludes with a powerful affirmation of faith's role in transcending fear. By recognizing fear as faith placed in the wrong kingdom, we can consciously choose to place our trust in God's promises, leading to a life characterized by peace and purpose, aligned with divine destiny.

CHAPTER 18

THE BATTLEFIELD OF THE MIND

Bible Verse

2 Corinthians 10:3-5 - "For though we walk in the flesh, we do not war according to the flesh, for the weapons of our warfare are not of the flesh, but divinely powerful for the destruction of fortresses."

Introduction

This chapter discusses the spiritual warfare that believers face in their minds, emphasizing the necessity of recognizing and combating demonic influences that present themselves as destructive thoughts.

Word of Wisdom

"The battle for your future begins in your mind." Kris Vallotton

Main Theme

Spiritual warfare primarily manifests in the mind, where believers must vigilantly guard against the enemy's attempts to plant destructive thoughts.

Key Points

- Spiritual battles often occur when believers attempt to advance into new spiritual territories.
- Demonic forces aim to implant negative thoughts in our minds, challenging our identity in Christ.
- Recognizing these thoughts as external attacks is crucial to maintaining spiritual health.
- The Apostle Paul teaches that spiritual warfare requires divine power, not just human effort.
- Successfully managing our thoughts involves capturing them and aligning them with Christ's truth.

Key Themes

- **Understanding the Origin of Thoughts:** It is essential for believers to discern the source of their thoughts, distinguishing between their own and those implanted by demonic forces, to avoid falling into spiritual traps.
- **Strategic Response to Spiritual Attacks:** By identifying and rejecting demonic thoughts, believers can prevent

these ideas from taking root and forming strongholds that oppose God's will.

- **The Role of Faith in Overcoming Fear:** Maintaining faith in God's power rather than succumbing to fear is a crucial strategy in spiritual warfare, transforming fear into fortitude.

- **Importance of Scriptural Meditation:** Regular meditation on the Scriptures equips believers with the truth needed to counteract the lies and accusations of the enemy.

- **Proactive Spiritual Discipline:** Actively taking every thought captive under Christ's authority is not just defensive but a proactive measure in maintaining spiritual clarity and peace.

Conclusion

This chapter concludes with encouragement for believers to remain vigilant in the spiritual battle for their minds, using the weapons of divine truth and righteousness to dismantle the enemy's schemes and fortify their spiritual wellbeing.

CHAPTER 19

FAILING FORWARD

Bible Verse

Proverbs 24:16 - "For a righteous person falls seven times and rises again, but the wicked stumble in time of disaster."

Introduction

This chapter explores the concept of learning from failures, emphasizing the difference between experiencing failure and embodying it as an identity.

Word of Wisdom

"I just spent thousands of dollars on your education!" - Highlighting the value of learning from failures rather than penalizing them.

Main Theme

The chapter discusses how failure is not a defining factor but a stepping stone to greater wisdom and success when approached with the right mindset.

Key Points

- Both Judas and Peter failed Jesus, but their responses to their failures dramatically shaped their destinies.
- Recognizing and owning up to failures can provide valuable learning experiences.
- It is crucial to differentiate between failing in an act and becoming a failure in identity.
- Learning from failures can prevent the repetition of the same mistakes.
- Taking responsibility for failures allows for personal and professional growth.

Key Themes

- **The Learning Process in Failure:** An honest evaluation of one's role in failures facilitates learning and growth, preventing the recurrence of similar mistakes in the future.
- **The Impact of Acknowledgment:** By acknowledging mistakes and learning from them, individuals can transform potential negative experiences into opportunities for development and success.
- **Risk and Reward:** Embracing risks is essential for growth; failures should be

seen as part of the learning curve that leads to eventual success.

- **Long-term Benefits of Embracing Failures:** Viewing failures as investments in personal education can lead to improved strategies and resilience in future endeavors.
- **The Role of Forgiveness in Failure:** Forgiving oneself and learning from failures can lead to a healthier, forward-moving life perspective, avoiding the stagnation that comes with dwelling on past mistakes.

Conclusion

Emphasizing the importance of moving forward from failures with lessons learned, the chapter encourages readers to view each failure as a stepping stone towards success, reshaping their approach to risk and personal growth.

CHAPTER 20

THE DARK NIGHT OF THE FLESH

Bible Verse

Matthew 6:25-34 - "Therefore I tell you, do not be anxious about your life..."

Introduction

This chapter delves into the complexities of human nature—spirit, soul, and body— and the challenges we face when any part is out of balance. It discusses the stigmatization and potential benefits of antidepressants, the physiological factors influencing mental health, and holistic strategies to combat depression and anxiety.

Word of Wisdom

"My wife got sick of me being depressed and insisted that I do something!" - A candid reflection on the

turning point that led to seeking medical help for depression.

Main Theme

The discussion centers on understanding and addressing the multifaceted aspects of mental health, emphasizing the physical, environmental, and spiritual factors that contribute to our overall well-being.

Key Points

- Human beings are complex, with interconnected spiritual, emotional, and physical needs.
- Depression and anxiety can stem from chemical imbalances that may require medical intervention.
- Lifestyle factors significantly impact mental health, including sleep, sunlight exposure, stress levels, and physical activity.
- Antidepressants can play a crucial role in stabilizing mood and improving quality of life.
- Seeking professional help and adjusting lifestyle factors can lead to substantial improvements in mental health.

Key Themes

- **Interconnection of Body, Mind, and Spirit:** The health of one aspect affects the others; imbalances can lead to severe mental health challenges, but addressing these can restore harmony and functionality.
- **Role of Medication in Mental Health:** Medication should not be stigmatized but seen as a potentially essential component in the toolkit for managing severe depressive and anxious symptoms, providing stability while underlying issues are addressed.
- **Importance of Environmental Factors:** Sunlight, exercise, and reduced stress are not just lifestyle choices but necessities for maintaining serotonin levels and overall mental health, demonstrating how our modern lifestyle can be detrimental to our natural state.
- **Cultural Impact on Mental Health:** The modern world's demands can overwhelm the human psyche, necessitating intentional actions to preserve mental health such as disconnecting from continuous digital communication and focusing on restorative activities.
- **Personal Responsibility and Proactivity:** While medication can help, individuals must actively engage in practices that reduce stress and increase resilience, such as exercising, maintaining a

healthy sleep schedule, and seeking sunlight exposure.

Conclusion

The chapter encourages readers to adopt a holistic approach to mental health, which includes recognizing when medical intervention is needed, adjusting lifestyle factors, and understanding the intricate balance between our physical environment and mental state.

CHAPTER 21

SLEEPING BEAUTY

Bible Verse

Psalm 4:6-8 - "In peace I will both lie down and
sleep, for You alone, Lord, make me dwell in
safety."

Introduction

This chapter emphasizes the critical importance of sleep in maintaining mental, emotional, and spiritual health. The author shares personal experiences and scientific insights to underscore sleep's role in fostering overall well-being.

Word of Wisdom

"I just spent thousands of dollars on your education!" - A perspective on embracing failures as learning opportunities,

reflective of the author's optimistic and growth-oriented mindset.

Main Theme

The necessity of sleep is explored not just as a physical requirement but as a spiritual and emotional rejuvenator, essential for optimal functioning and health.

Key Points

- Sleep is essential for mental, emotional, and spiritual well-being.
- Sleep deprivation significantly impacts mood, cognitive function, and overall health.
- Medication may be necessary to manage sleep disturbances, especially during periods of acute stress.
- Professional help can be crucial in addressing underlying causes of sleep deprivation.
- Lifestyle adjustments, including managing light exposure and stress, are vital for improving sleep quality.
- The spiritual dimension of sleep involves restoration and divine communication during rest.

Key Themes

- **Understanding Sleep's Impact:** Sleep affects every aspect of our well-being, and chronic deprivation can lead to severe mental and physical health issues. Addressing sleep issues is not just about feeling rested but about maintaining balance and health in every part of life.

- **Medical and Spiritual Approaches to Sleep:** Combining medical interventions with spiritual practices can enhance sleep quality. Medications might be necessary to stabilize sleep patterns, while spiritual practices can enrich the quality of rest and the insights gained from dreams.

- **Role of Lifestyle in Sleep Quality:** Modern lifestyles often disrupt natural sleep patterns, necessitating intentional changes to reclaim healthy sleep. This includes managing technology use, ensuring physical activity, and creating a conducive sleeping environment.

- **Sleep as a Spiritual Experience:** Sleep provides an opportunity for spiritual renewal and divine encounters. Understanding sleep's spiritual dimension can transform our approach to rest, seeing it not as downtime but as a sacred space for growth and rejuvenation.

- **Proactive Sleep Management:** Encouraging proactive management of sleep through medical consultation and lifestyle adjustments demonstrates the need to prioritize sleep as a foundational aspect of health and spiritual well-being.

Conclusion

The chapter serves as a compelling call to action to prioritize sleep as a pillar of health, integrating medical, lifestyle, and spiritual strategies to combat the pervasive issue of sleep deprivation in modern society.

CHAPTER 22

VISION GIVES PAIN A PURPOSE

Bible Verse

Proverbs 29:18 - "Where there is no vision, the people are unrestrained, but happy is one who keeps the Law."

Introduction

This chapter explores how having a vision transforms challenges into opportunities for growth and meaning. Using the metaphor of Michelangelo seeing an angel in the marble, the author illustrates how vision can give purpose to the pain we experience in life.

Word of Wisdom

"The difference between chipping rock and freeing angels is what we see or envision in the stone of our lives." Kris Vallotton

. . .

Main Theme

The significance of having a vision is emphasized as a transformative tool that turns ordinary and painful experiences into powerful and purposeful actions, aligning personal goals with divine intentions.

Key Points

- Vision transforms challenges into opportunities and guides actions toward meaningful outcomes.
- Without vision, people lack restraint and purpose, leading to aimless or destructive behaviors.
- Vision helps to endure and contextualize pain, turning it into a sign of growth.
- Maintaining a vision requires discipline and adherence to certain principles or "laws."
- Jesus' endurance of the crucifixion, motivated by the vision of resurrection, serves as the ultimate example.
- Physical representations like gym mirrors help maintain focus on vision by providing immediate feedback.

Key Themes

- **Vision as a Catalyst for Growth:** Vision not only guides individuals through pain but also fuels personal growth and discipline. It enables people to focus on long-term goals rather than immediate discomfort, thus fostering resilience and perseverance.

- **The Role of Vision in Spiritual and Physical Realms:** In both spiritual pursuits and physical endeavors like fitness, vision provides a roadmap that directs efforts and sustains motivation. It is crucial in overcoming the natural resistance encountered in any growth process.
- **Transformative Power of Vision:** Vision has the power to redefine painful experiences, turning them into opportunities for strength and renewal. This transformative ability highlights the importance of having a clear, positive outlook on future goals.
- **Vision and Identity:** A strong vision helps to shape one's identity in alignment with one's aspirations and values. It acts as a buffer against negative influences and reinforces a positive self-image and life purpose.
- **Endurance Fueled by Vision:** Just as athletes endure pain during training to achieve physical goals, individuals can endure life's challenges more effectively when they are anchored by a clear and compelling vision. This endurance is essential for achieving significant life goals.

Conclusion

The chapter concludes by emphasizing the importance of maintaining a vision that aligns with divine purpose, which not only imbues difficult experiences with meaning but also propels individuals toward fulfilling their true potential. The narrative encourages readers to identify and pursue their visions with tenacity and faith, transforming their lives into powerful testimonies of growth and achievement.

CHAPTER 23

HOPE: YOU CAN LEARN FROM RATS

Bible Verse

Romans 8:28 - "We know that God causes all things to work together for good to those who love God, to those who are called according to His purpose."

Introduction

This chapter examines the profound impact of hope on perseverance and endurance, drawing inspiration from an experiment with rats by Dr. Curt Paul Richter. It posits that hope significantly extends our capacity to cope with challenges by providing a mental and emotional boost.

Word of Wisdom

"Hope is not about circumstances; it's about perspective, the way you view situations." Kris Vallotton

Main Theme

The central theme of this chapter is the transformative power of hope in extending human endurance and resilience. The narrative uses the example of rats swimming dramatically longer when given a glimpse of rescue to illustrate how hope can energize and sustain us through difficult times.

Key Points

- Dr. Richter's experiment showed rats swimming longer when given hope, highlighting hope's role in enhancing endurance.
- Solomon's insights from Proverbs 13:12 emphasize that lacking vision or hope leads to aimlessness and despair.
- Hope empowers people to press through difficult circumstances, attracting faith that can visualize unseen outcomes.
- The chapter underscores the importance of maintaining hope as a strategy to enhance life's challenges.
- Hope is described as an expectation of good, which energizes and motivates us even in dire situations.

Key Themes

- **Empirical Evidence of Hope:** The experiments by Dr. Richter serve as empirical evidence that hope can dramatically improve endurance and effort in challenging situations. This provides a compelling argument for the psychological benefits of having hope.

- **Biblical Perspective on Hope:** The Biblical viewpoint, particularly through Solomon's and Paul's writings, supports the notion that vision and hope prevent spiritual and emotional stagnation and propel individuals towards fulfilling their divine purpose.
- **Hope as an Energizer:** Hope acts as an energizer that not only prolongs physical activity, as seen in the rats, but also enhances emotional and spiritual endurance in humans. It changes our perception of our capabilities and limits.
- **The Necessity of Vision:** Vision is crucial as it directs our efforts and sustains our spirits. Without vision, people lack the restraint necessary to channel their energies effectively towards achieving meaningful goals.
- **Transformative Impact of Hope:** Hope transforms our response to pain and adversity. By envisioning a positive outcome, hope allows individuals to endure pain with a purpose, much like athletes endure physical discomfort to achieve greater fitness.

Conclusion

The chapter concludes by affirming that hope is essential for overcoming life's challenges. It encourages readers to cultivate a hopeful perspective, not as a naïve dismissal of reality, but as a strategic approach to life that acknowledges and utilizes the intrinsic link between vision, hope, and endurance. This perspective not only changes how we handle present difficulties but also how we shape our future.

CHAPTER 24

GET VACCINATED

Bible Verse

1 Thessalonians 5:16-18 - "Rejoice always, pray without ceasing, in everything give thanks; for this is the will of God for you in Christ Jesus."

Introduction

This chapter delves into the transformative power of gratitude, using a personal dream as a metaphor for being inoculated against negative emotions. The author shares how embracing gratitude shifted his perspective and alleviated the burdens of various crises.

Word of Wisdom

"It's impossible to be thankful and arrogant at the same time, because gratitude is a manifestation of humility." Kris Vallotton

Main Theme

The main theme revolves around the concept of gratitude acting as a spiritual vaccine against bitterness, resentment, and other negative states, transforming challenges into opportunities for growth and spiritual renewal.

Key Points

- The author had a vivid dream about being vaccinated with gratitude, which marked a turning point in his life.
- Gratitude helped the author navigate through personal and community crises, including church leadership challenges and personal grief.
- Regular practice of gratitude shifted the author's focus from despair to hope, significantly improving his mental health.
- The exercise of listing daily gratitudes, though initially challenging, became a crucial tool for mental and emotional resilience.
- Scripture supports the practice of gratitude as essential for spiritual well-being and resilience in the face of trials.

Key Themes

- **Gratitude as Spiritual Resilience:** Gratitude not only counteracts negative emotions but also fortifies the spirit against future hardships. It transforms how we perceive and react to life's challenges, enabling us to find joy and purpose in adversity.

- **The Transformative Power of a Gratitude Practice:** Implementing a daily practice of gratitude can profoundly affect one's mental state, turning overwhelming stress into manageable challenges and changing one's outlook on life from victimhood to empowerment.
- **Biblical Foundations for Gratitude:** The teachings of Paul in Thessalonians emphasize the importance of gratitude in all circumstances, reinforcing that it is God's will for us to find joy and thankfulness regardless of our external conditions.
- **Practical Applications of Gratitude:** The daily act of writing down things one is thankful for serves as a practical application of biblical teachings, promoting a continual awareness of God's ongoing work in our lives.
- **Gratitude Amid Crisis:** During the toughest times, gratitude acts as a key to unlocking peace and perspective, providing a pathway out of darkness and into a place where one can thrive despite difficulties.

Conclusion

"Get Vaccinated" serves as a compelling narrative about the necessity of gratitude in overcoming life's inevitable challenges. It encourages readers to adopt a habit of thankfulness, which aligns with biblical commands and promises significant shifts in personal well-being and spiritual growth. This chapter is a call to actively practice gratitude, transforming trials into triumphs through the power of a positive, faith-filled outlook.

CHAPTER 25

I WILL SAVE YOU

Bible Verse

Matthew 11:28-30 - "Come to Me, all who are weary and heavy-laden, and I will give you rest. Take My yoke upon you and learn from Me, for I am gentle and humble in heart, and YOU WILL FIND REST FOR YOUR SOULS. For My yoke is easy and My burden is light."

Introduction

This chapter explores the dangers of taking on the savior role in other people's lives, using personal stories of family crises to highlight the necessity of entrusting others to God's care.

Word of Wisdom

"You are not the savior of the world!"
- a divine reminder received during a pe-

riod of intense personal crisis. Kris
Vallotton

Main Theme

The focus is on the importance of recognizing our limitations in helping others and the need to hand over the reins to God, who is the true restorer and savior.

Key Points

• The author experienced intense personal crises, feeling responsible for rescuing his family from their struggles.

• He learned a critical lesson about the dangers of assuming the role of a savior.

• God's intervention reminded him of his human limitations and the need to trust in divine providence.

• Setting healthy boundaries is essential to maintain one's well-being and effectiveness in helping others.

• Suffering sometimes serves as a necessary catalyst for personal growth and reliance on God.

Key Themes

• **Misplaced Savior Complex:** Taking on a savior role for others can lead to personal burnout and detracts from God's role in their lives. Recognizing and admitting this can prevent many emotional and spiritual pitfalls.

- **Divine Boundaries:** It is vital to understand where our responsibilities end and where we must allow God to intervene. This understanding can lead to healthier relationships and personal peace.
- **The Necessity of Surrender:** Surrendering control to God is not a sign of weakness but of wisdom, acknowledging that some situations are beyond human ability to fix and require divine intervention.
- **Spiritual Responsibility:** While we are called to love and serve others, we must do so with the understanding that we are not their saviors. Our role is to support, not to supplant God in their lives.
- **Hope in Divine Restoration:** The belief that God can manage our burdens better than we can is fundamental to Christian faith. This trust allows us to live freely and serve others without being overwhelmed.

Conclusion

"I Will Save You" imparts a crucial lesson on the importance of recognizing our human limits and the transformative power of placing our trust in God's hands. It encourages readers to focus on supporting rather than saving, thus fulfilling our true calling under God's sovereignty.

CHAPTER 26

BOUNDARIES

Bible Verse

Matthew 14:23 - "After He had sent the crowds away, He went up on the mountain by Himself to pray; and when it was evening, He was there alone."

Introduction

The chapter delves into the necessity of setting boundaries to maintain personal well-being and effectiveness in ministry, using the author's experiences at Bethel Church as a backdrop.

Word of Wisdom

"Personally, I am learning to love the sound of my feet walking away from things not meant for me." Kris Vallotton

Main Theme

Boundaries are essential for healthy relationships and personal sanity. They help preserve our energy and ensure we are only engaging in responsibilities that align with our divine purpose.

Key Points

• The author struggled with overwhelming ministry demands until he established firm boundaries.

• Misplaced priorities can lead to burnout and ineffectiveness.

• It's crucial to identify one's strengths and weaknesses to maximize impact.

• Not everyone will understand or respect your boundaries, which can lead to feelings of guilt or conflict.

• Setting boundaries is not just beneficial; it's necessary for maintaining one's health and spiritual well-being.

Key Themes

- **Understanding Capacity:** Recognizing personal limits is crucial; it involves discerning what one is capable of handling and knowing when to say no. This self-awareness protects from overcommitment and stress.
- **Dealing with Disappointment:** Part of setting boundaries is managing the negative reactions of others. It requires

staying firm in one's convictions despite potential backlash or misunderstanding.

- **Spiritual and Personal Refreshment:** Just as Jesus separated Himself to connect with God, setting boundaries helps maintain spiritual vitality. It allows for times of refreshment and communion with God.
- **Avoiding the Savior Complex:** It's important to differentiate between being helpful and taking on a savior role. Over-responsibility for others' well-being can lead to personal and spiritual demise.
- **Strategic Engagement:** Focus on engaging in activities and relationships where one can have the most impact. This involves saying no to situations where one's contribution might be minimal or counterproductive.

Conclusion

"Boundaries" teaches that knowing when to engage and when to step back is crucial for anyone in a caregiving or ministerial role. It emphasizes that true compassion sometimes involves guiding others to help beyond what we can provide, echoing Jesus' example of balancing ministry with personal boundaries for renewal and connection with God.

CHAPTER 27

QUESTION REALITY

Bible Verse

John 8:31-32 - "So Jesus was saying to those Jews who had believed Him, 'If you continue in My word, then you are truly My disciples; and you will know the truth, and the truth will set you free.'"

Introduction

This chapter explores the profound importance of questioning the lenses through which we perceive reality, emphasizing how our core values and past experiences shape our understanding of the world.

Word of Wisdom

"I finally determined that I would believe the Bible and doubt my fears." Kris Vallotton

Main Theme

Understanding and adjusting our core values are crucial for accurately perceiving reality, which is vital for living in true freedom as defined by Christ.

Key Points

• Perception is often clouded by past experiences and core values, which can distort reality.

• Our responses and interpretations of life are filtered through the 'lenses' of our core values.

• Incorrect core values can lead to a life based on distorted perceptions and decisions.

• The Bible is a crucial tool for realigning our perceptions with the truth.

• Changing our core values based on truth can transform our approach to life and relationships.

Key Themes

- **Impact of Core Values:** Core values act like lenses or instruments, shaping our perception of every situation. If these are flawed or distorted, our entire outlook on life can be skewed, leading us away from truth.
- **The Danger of Misguided Perceptions:** Relying on distorted perceptions can have catastrophic effects, similar to a pilot experiencing spatial disorientation. This analogy underscores

the importance of aligning our core values with truth rather than subjective feelings.

- **The Role of the Bible in Reality:** Engaging with the Bible helps clarify our vision, acting like a corrective lens that aligns our perception with God's reality. This spiritual discipline transforms our internal narrative and external interactions.
- **Healing from Past Traumas:** Recognizing how past traumas and unresolved issues cloud perception is the first step towards healing. True healing involves acknowledging these distortions and seeking truth in God's word.
- **Practical Steps to Adjust Core Values:** The chapter encourages active engagement with Scripture and intentional reflection on personal biases and the sources of those biases, promoting a journey towards clearer, more truthful perception.

Conclusion

"Question Reality" challenges readers to examine and adjust the foundational beliefs that influence their understanding of the world. By aligning these core values with biblical truth, individuals can experience genuine freedom and a more accurate perception of the world around them, leading to healthier interactions and decisions.

CHAPTER 28

ISSUES OF THE HEART

Bible Verse

Romans 10:9-10 - "If you confess with your mouth
Jesus as Lord, and believe in your heart that God
raised Him from the dead, you will be saved; for
with the heart a person believes, resulting in
righteousness, and with the mouth he confesses,
resulting in salvation."

Introduction

This chapter delves into the distinction
between high values and core values, illustrating the importance of aligning beliefs
held intellectually (high values) with those truly
integrated into our heart (core values).

Word of Wisdom

*"Core values are only effective when I
actually believe them with my heart, not*

just agree with them with my head." Kris Vallotton

Main Theme

Understanding and reconciling the gap between our professed values and our deeply held beliefs is essential for genuine personal growth and spiritual health.

Key Points

• High values are ideals we hold dear, whereas core values are the truths that govern our actual perceptions and behaviors.

• There is often a disconnect between what we claim to value and what we truly embrace at a deeper level.

• This incongruity can lead to significant life challenges and internal conflicts.

• The process of integrating high values into core beliefs involves intentional practice and repetition.

• Failure in this integration process is common, but persistence is key to success.

Key Themes

• **Defining High vs. Core Values:** High values are intellectual or superficial beliefs, whereas core values are those that drive our deepest motivations and reactions.

Recognizing the difference helps us address inconsistencies in our lives.

- **Aligning Values with Actions:** To truly integrate high values into core values, one must not only understand and agree with a value but also live it out until it becomes second nature, a concept akin to developing "faith muscle memory."
- **The Role of Scripture in Value Formation:** Meditating on and confessing scripture helps solidify our core values, aligning our heart and mind with biblical truths, thus enabling a life lived in accordance with God's will.
- **The Importance of Genuine Belief:** Believing something with one's heart rather than just intellectually agreeing with it transforms high values into core values, impacting how we view and interact with the world.
- **Practical Steps to Value Integration:** The chapter provides a five-step process to develop healthy core values, emphasizing discovery, memorization, meditation, practice, and repetition to ensure deep integration.

Conclusion

"Issues of the Heart" challenges readers to examine the authenticity of their beliefs, encouraging a journey from mere intellectual agreement to heartfelt conviction. Through a methodical process of introspection and application, one can align their core values with their actions, leading to a more integrated and fulfilling life.

CHAPTER 29

THE PLANE TRUTH

Bible Verse

2 Timothy 1:7 NKJV - "For God has not given us a spirit of fear, but of power and of love and of a sound mind."

Introduction

This chapter explores the concept of fear and its impact on limiting our life's potential. It encourages confronting fears directly to expand one's capacity to live fully and courageously.

Word of Wisdom

"Courage is fear that has said its prayers!" Kris Vallotton

Main Theme

Fear often constrains us to a comfort zone far smaller than our capabilities and destinies. This chapter challenges us to recognize and confront these fears to reclaim and expand our lives.

Key Points

• Fear often leads to self-imposed limitations, reducing life's potential activities and experiences.

• Overcoming fear involves moving from avoidance to confrontation, even if it means feeling uncomfortable.

• Real courage is demonstrated when one faces their fears, not by avoiding them.

• Support from others can be crucial in overcoming debilitating fears.

• Regularly facing fears incrementally can restore normalcy and confidence over time.

Key Themes

- **Recognizing Fear as a Limitation:** Fear is not just an emotion but a barrier that keeps us from fulfilling our potential. Recognizing this can be the first step toward overcoming these limitations.
- **The Role of Support in Overcoming Fear:** The encouragement and insistence of others can be crucial in helping us take the first steps towards confronting our fears, as illustrated by the author's personal experience with his wife's support.

- **Incremental Exposure to Fear:**
  Gradually exposing oneself to fearful
  situations can desensitize and reclaim the
  freedoms fear has taken away, much like
  gradually increasing doses of a vaccine to
  build immunity.
- **Scriptural Empowerment Against
  Fear:** The Bible provides numerous verses
  that offer strength and perspective against
  fear, suggesting that divine truth is a
  powerful antidote to fear.
- **Actionable Steps to Combat Fear:** The
  chapter provides practical steps for readers
  to identify their fears, imagine bold
  actions, and then take concrete steps to act
  despite their fears, using scriptural
  meditations as support.

Conclusion

"The Plane Truth" serves as a powerful reminder
that living fully requires confronting fears with
faith and action. By recognizing and systematically
challenging the fears that limit us, we can expand
our horizons and fulfill our divine destinies.

CHAPTER 30

THE POWER OF NOBILITY

Bible Verse

1 Corinthians 10:13 - "No temptation has overtaken you except something common to mankind; and God is faithful, so He will not allow you to be tempted beyond what you are able, but with the temptation will provide the way of escape also, so that you will be able to endure it."

Introduction

This chapter explores the concept of nobility as an internal quality strengthened by overcoming temptations and challenges, rather than succumbing to them.

Word of Wisdom

"Nobility is actually tested and grown in a culture of temptation." Kris Vallotton

Main Theme

Nobility is defined not by one's ability to avoid temptation, but through the strength of character that resists and manages these temptations effectively.

Key Points

• Nobility is about the virtues we embrace rather than the temptations we resist.

• Facing temptations can strengthen character and increase nobility.

• Misunderstanding nobility can lead to a misalignment between values and actions.

• Overcoming fears and expanding life experiences can restore normalcy and confidence.

• Nobility involves managing one's fears and actions in alignment with inner values.

Key Themes

- **Character Strength through Adversity:** True nobility is demonstrated through actions, particularly how one handles temptations and challenges. Resisting temptations like dishonesty or infidelity strengthens one's moral and ethical foundations.
- **Cultural and Personal Misconceptions of Nobility:** Modern misconceptions can lead to a skewed

understanding of what it means to be noble. This chapter clarifies that nobility involves a steadfast adherence to moral convictions, regardless of external pressures or temptations.

- **The Role of Core Values in Defining Nobility:** Core values are crucial in defining one's actions and responses to various life situations. They serve as the lens through which we view and interact with the world.
- **Misalignment Between Professed and Actual Beliefs:** There is often a disconnect between what people claim to value and what they truly hold dear, as demonstrated through their actions especially under pressure.
- **Practical Steps Towards Embracing Nobility:** The chapter outlines actionable steps to align one's professed beliefs with their core values, emphasizing the importance of consistency between belief and action.

Conclusion

"The Power of Nobility" encourages readers to reassess their internal values and align their actions with these principles to lead a truly noble life. It urges an introspective look at how one deals with temptations and challenges, advocating for integrity and strength of character in all aspects of life.

CHAPTER 31

LEADERSHIP

Bible Verse

1 Corinthians 4:15-17 - "For if you were to have countless tutors in Christ, yet you would not have many fathers, for in Christ Jesus I became your father through the gospel. Therefore I urge you, be imitators of me. For this reason I have sent to you Timothy, who is my beloved and faithful child in the Lord, and he will remind you of my ways which are in Christ, just as I teach everywhere in every church."

Introduction

This chapter highlights the transformative power of spiritual leadership through discipleship, illustrated by a personal testimony of finding faith and guidance.

Word of Wisdom

"Jesus never told us to make Chris-

tians; He taught us to make disciples."
Kris Vallotton

Main Theme

The essential role of spiritual parenting in personal and communal growth within the Christian faith, emphasizing the need for mature guidance in spiritual journeys.

Key Points

• Spiritual leadership was crucial in the author's personal journey to faith.

• Discipleship is defined not just by learning but also by personal guidance and mentorship.

• Effective leaders inspire by action and personal integrity, not just by title.

• Spiritual parents play a pivotal role in nurturing and guiding spiritual growth.

• Establishing core values in discipleship is essential for developing strong faith foundations.

Key Themes

• **Importance of Spiritual Parenting:**
  The concept of spiritual parenting is
  crucial in guiding individuals through their

faith journey, offering not just teaching but also loving care and mentorship.

- **Transformation Through Discipleship:** True transformation in faith comes from the consistent and loving input of seasoned believers who invest personally and spiritually in others' lives.
- **Personal Testimony as a Teaching Tool:** Sharing personal experiences and struggles can be a powerful way to lead and teach, providing relatable and practical examples of living a faith-filled life.
- **The Challenge of Spiritual Leadership:** Spiritual leadership involves significant challenges, including the need for personal integrity and the wisdom to manage both personal and community expectations.
- **Reconciling Head Knowledge with Heart Belief:** There is often a gap between intellectual agreement with spiritual truths and true heart belief; effective discipleship bridges this gap.

Conclusion

The chapter on Leadership emphasizes the transformative impact of spiritual mentors, illustrating how genuine, caring leadership can significantly alter life paths and deepen faith. It calls for a reevaluation of personal spiritual leadership roles and encourages seeking or becoming mentors who genuinely reflect Christ's teachings.

CHAPTER 32

PRESENT AND ACCOUNTED FOR

Bible Verse

Genesis 28:10-17 - "Then Jacob awoke from his sleep and said, 'Surely the Lord is in this place, and I did not know it.'"

Introduction

This chapter reflects on the importance of being present in the moment to fully engage with God's plans and the people around us. It discusses how being mentally absent can cause us to miss divine encounters and meaningful connections.

Word of Wisdom

"You are never really here. I've planned for you to have encounters with Me throughout the day, but you miss most

of them because you are never really here."
Kris Vallotton

Main Theme

The necessity of mindfulness and presence in our daily lives to experience the fullness of God's presence and the richness of our relationships.

Key Points

• Being present enhances our ability to connect with others and experience God's presence.

• Distractions and mental absence can cause us to miss important moments and interactions.

• Mindfulness is a practice that requires intentional effort and focus.

• Living in the moment allows us to appreciate life's details and divine appointments.

• The journey to becoming fully present is challenging but rewarding.

Key Themes

• **Impact of Mindfulness on Relationships:** Being fully present not only strengthens our relationships but also deepens our empathy and understanding towards others. It transforms ordinary interactions into meaningful exchanges.

- **Divine Encounters in Daily Moments:** By staying mindful, we open ourselves to recognizing God's presence in everyday situations, much like Jacob's unexpected revelation in a seemingly ordinary place.
- **Challenges of Modern Distractions:** In an era of constant connectivity, learning to be present is both a counter-cultural and a deeply spiritual act, requiring us to consciously disconnect from distractions to engage with the real.
- **Personal Growth Through Presence:** Mindfulness and presence are not just spiritual practices but are also essential for personal growth, allowing us to live more fulfilled and less anxious lives.
- **The Continuous Practice of Mindfulness:** Being present is a continual practice that involves regular self-reflection, discipline, and the willingness to engage fully with the present moment, regardless of its nature.

Conclusion

The chapter "Present and Accounted For" calls for a deliberate effort to engage with the present moment, advocating for a life lived fully aware and deeply connected to both divine presence and human relationships. It challenges readers to rethink their daily interactions and the quality of their attention to life's details.

CHAPTER 33

THE POWER OF FRIENDSHIP

Bible Verse

Ecclesiastes 4:9-12 - "Two are better than one because they have a good return for their labor; for if either of them falls, the one will lift up his companion."

Introduction

This chapter explores the profound impact of friendship on overcoming life's challenges, emphasizing the necessity of community and mutual support through difficult times, as illustrated by personal anecdotes and scriptural wisdom.

Word of Wisdom

"When we're struggling in life, we must draw close to people and draw strength and grace from them." Kris Vallotton

Main Theme

The essential role of friendship in navigating life's tribulations, providing support, and enhancing resilience.

Key Points

• Friendship provides critical support during personal crises.

• Isolation can exacerbate struggles and lengthen recovery.

• Genuine friends offer hope and practical help.

• Community is vital for emotional and spiritual health.

• Proactive engagement in friendships enriches life.

Key Themes

- **Support During Trials:** True friends are pivotal during life's lowest points, offering emotional and sometimes physical support that can be life-saving.
- **Counteracting Isolation:** In a culture that often shuns vulnerability, having friends who understand and share our burdens can significantly ease emotional distress and promote healing.
- **Influence of Healthy Friendships:** Surrounding ourselves with positive, faith-filled individuals can uplift us and provide

the courage needed to face life's challenges.

- **Biblical Perspective on Companionship:** Scripture supports the concept of communal living and mutual support, highlighting the practical and spiritual benefits of having reliable companions.
- **Proactivity in Cultivating Relationships:** The importance of nurturing and investing in friendships is emphasized as a proactive measure to ensure we have the support network needed during times of crisis.

Conclusion

"The Power of Friendship" underscores that life is not meant to be navigated alone. Friends are not only essential for personal growth but are a fundamental aspect of living a fulfilled and resilient life. By embracing and nurturing our relationships, we prepare ourselves not only to receive support but also to give it, fulfilling one of our most significant roles in each other's lives.

CHAPTER 34

ONLY THE LONELY

Bible Verse

John 15:13 - "Greater love has no one than this, that a person will lay down his life for his friends."

Introduction

This chapter addresses the pervasive issue of loneliness, emphasizing the importance of cultivating meaningful relationships and the detrimental effects of isolation.

Word of Wisdom

"Some of us are laying down our friends for our lives, instead of laying down our lives for our friends—and then we wonder why we're so lonely!" Kris Vallotton

Main Theme

The critical need for authentic human connections in combatting loneliness and fostering a fulfilling life.

Key Points

• Loneliness is a significant modern-day epidemic.

• Authentic relationships are essential for emotional health.

• Proactive steps are necessary to overcome isolation.

• Friendship involves both giving and receiving support.

• Building relationships requires intentional effort.

Key Themes

- **Impact of Technology on Social Interaction:** Modern technology, while connecting us digitally, often leads to a physical and emotional disconnect, contributing to the loneliness epidemic.
- **The Importance of Presence in Relationships:** True connections are formed through presence and genuine interaction, not through passive engagements like listening to music or playing video games.
- **Proactive Relationship Building:** To combat loneliness, individuals must take deliberate actions such as reaching out,

sharing experiences, and participating in community activities.

- **The Role of Vulnerability in Friendship:** Opening up to others about our struggles and accepting their support is crucial in building strong, supportive relationships.
- **Societal Attitudes towards Pain and Support:** Our society often shuns the display of pain and vulnerability, but acknowledging and sharing our struggles with trusted friends can lead to healing and strengthened bonds.

Conclusion

"Only the Lonely" highlights the profound impact of loneliness on mental health and the transformative power of friendship. By understanding the value of companionship and actively seeking meaningful relationships, we can enhance our well-being and lead richer, more connected lives.

CHAPTER 35

FINDING RHYTHM

Bible Verse

2 Timothy 3:10-14 - "Now you followed my teaching, conduct, purpose, faith, patience, love, perseverance, persecutions, and sufferings, such as happened to me at Antioch, at Iconium, and at Lystra; what persecutions I endured, and out of them all the Lord rescued me!"

Introduction

This chapter explores the concept of rhythm in life, comparing it to music that flows with purpose and harmony. It challenges the reader to consider whether their life is a melody or just noise, urging a reflection on the structure and direction of their daily existence.

Word of Wisdom

"Music is noise submitted to rules; life

without rhythm is just noise." Kris Vallotton

Main Theme

The importance of establishing a purposeful rhythm in life that aligns with one's core values and God's plan, much like music which requires structure and harmony to resonate beautifully.

Key Points

• Life, like music, requires a clear theme or purpose.

• Setting goals helps measure progress towards that purpose.

• Establishing a rhythm through consistent habits is crucial.

• Authenticity is key to maintaining one's unique life song.

• The dangers of living without a directed purpose include falling into noise and chaos.

Key Themes

• **Purpose and Theme:** Just as a song requires a theme to guide its melody, life needs a clear purpose to prevent it from descending into chaos. This purpose provides direction and motivation, making each action and decision part of a larger, coherent plan.

- **Goals and Measurement:** Goals function like musical scores that guide performance; they provide benchmarks against which one's progress towards their life's purpose can be measured, helping maintain focus and direction.
- **Rhythm and Habits:** Consistent, healthy habits are the rhythm section of life's music, creating a regular pattern that propels one forward towards their goals and keeps daily activities aligned with their overarching purpose.
- **Authenticity and Individuality:** Losing authenticity in life is akin to a musician playing out of tune; it results in a life that mimics others and lacks the unique melody intended by its creator. Living authentically means embracing and expressing one's true self without succumbing to external pressures.
- **The Conductor's Role:** Just as an orchestra needs a conductor to harmonize various instruments, individuals need guidance—whether divine or through wise counsel—to align their actions with their purpose and avoid discord in their life's music.

Conclusion

"Finding Rhythm" underlines the necessity of infusing life with purposeful rhythm, akin to composing a beautiful piece of music. By establishing clear goals, embracing consistent habits, and remaining true to oneself, one can ensure that their life not only sounds melodious but also resonates with profound purpose and joy.

CHAPTER 36

SUPERMAN DOESN'T SWEEP LEAVES

Bible Verse

Romans 8:14-17 - "For all who are being led by the Spirit of God, these are sons and daughters of God. For you have not received a spirit of slavery leading to fear again, but you have received a spirit of adoption as sons and daughters by which we cry out, 'Abba! Father!' The Spirit Himself testifies with our spirit that we are children of God, and if children, heirs also, heirs of God and fellow heirs with Christ, if indeed we suffer with Him so that we may also be glorified with Him."

Introduction

This chapter explores the concept of identity and purpose through the metaphor of Superman, emphasizing the importance of recognizing and living according to our God-given identities rather than being caught up in trivial tasks that don't align with our calling.

Word of Wisdom

"Superman doesn't sweep leaves! Knowing who you are saves you from the trivial." Kris Vallotton

Main Theme

The significance of understanding our identity in Christ as heirs to His kingdom, which should shape our actions and free us from the pressure of proving our worth through performance.

Key Points

• Realizing our identity helps us focus on tasks that align with our divine purpose.

• We should not waste energy on tasks that do not contribute to our identity in Christ.

• The enemy often attacks our identity to lead us into a performance-based life.

• We must live from our identity as children of God, not perform to earn that identity.

• Knowing our identity in Christ allows us to live with purpose and avoid trivial distractions.

Key Themes

• **Identity and Purpose:** Understanding our identity as children of God focuses us on what is truly important and aligns our actions with our divine purpose, preventing us from getting lost in unimportant tasks.

- **Performance vs. Identity:** The enemy tries to confuse our sense of self-worth with performance. Recognizing our identity in Christ enables us to live from a place of security and worth, not from a need to earn it through our actions.
- **Living Authentically:** When we know our true identity, we live authentically, fulfilling the unique roles God has for us rather than imitating others or meeting external expectations.
- **Overcoming the Performance Trap:** By rejecting the endless cycle of performance-based identity, we embrace a life of significance and peace, knowing our actions stem from our worth as God's heirs, not our efforts to prove our worth.
- **Strategic Living:** Embracing our identity in Christ allows us to strategically engage in activities that fulfill our calling, rather than being caught up in every demand or expectation placed upon us.

Conclusion

"Superman Doesn't Sweep Leaves" encourages readers to live a life grounded in the truth of their heavenly identity, enabling them to rise above the mundane and connect deeply with their divine purpose. By embracing our roles as God's heirs, we avoid the pitfalls of a performance-based lifestyle and engage more meaningfully with the world around us.

CHAPTER 37

FINDING YOUR SUPERPOWER

Bible Verse

Luke 9:1-2 - "He [Jesus] called the twelve together and gave them power and authority over all the demons, and the power to heal diseases. And He sent them out to proclaim the kingdom of God and to perform healing."

Introduction

This chapter inspires readers to recognize and embrace their God-given abilities, likened to superpowers, through the biblical story of Gideon. It encourages stepping out of fear and into faith, leveraging one's unique strengths for a divine purpose.

Word of Wisdom

"God sees more in you than you see in yourself. Embrace your divine superpower."
Kris Vallotton

Main Theme

The chapter emphasizes understanding and embracing the supernatural gifts and purpose God has bestowed upon us, urging readers to move beyond self-imposed limitations and fears.

Key Points

• Gideon's story illustrates transformation from fear to empowerment through divine calling.

• Self-doubt and low self-esteem can blind us to our potential and divine purpose.

• God equips the called, turning perceived weaknesses into strengths.

• Our 'superpowers' are the unique talents and abilities God has given us to fulfill His purpose.

• Overcoming fear and embracing faith are essential to activating our God-given potential.

Key Themes

- **Divine Empowerment:** Just as Gideon was called from a place of fear to lead with strength, each individual is equipped with unique capabilities meant to be used courageously for God's purposes.
- **Identity and Calling:** Recognizing and accepting our identity as God's chosen and empowered individuals enables us to live

out our calling effectively, without succumbing to the lies of inadequacy.

- **Transformation Through Faith:** Faith acts as a catalyst for transformation, turning ordinary individuals into extraordinary vessels of God's power, as illustrated by Gideon's victory with just 300 men.
- **The Impact of Divine Purpose:** Understanding our divine purpose helps focus our life's direction and actions, ensuring we use our talents in alignment with God's greater plan.
- **Challenging Self-Doubt:** By challenging our self-doubt and embracing our God-given identities, we can step into roles that may have seemed impossible, mirroring how Gideon overcame his insecurities to achieve greatness.

Conclusion

"Finding Your Superpower" compels readers to identify and utilize their unique strengths, or superpowers, in the service of God's plans. By shedding self-doubt and embracing faith, individuals can transform their lives and impact their world, much like Gideon did. This journey requires recognizing one's value and potential as ordained by God and actively stepping into the roles He has designed for us.

CHAPTER 38

LIVING BY FAITH

Bible Verse

Matthew 9:28-29 - "Jesus asked the blind men, 'Do you believe that I am able to do this?' 'Yes, Lord,' they replied. Then he touched their eyes and said, 'According to your faith let it be done to you.'"

Introduction

This chapter delves into the transformative power of faith in the believer's life, inspired by the story of Jesus healing two blind men based solely on their faith.

Word of Wisdom

"Faith is not just expecting great things from God; it is trusting God when we step into the great unknown." Kris Vallotton

Main Theme

The chapter challenges readers to examine the role of faith in their lives, emphasizing that faith is the primary component that can define and alter our reality and destiny.

Key Points

• Jesus' interaction with the blind men highlights the necessity of faith for miracles.

• Faith requires more than passive belief; it demands active expression and courage.

• Our understanding of God's promises directly influences the manifestation of His power in our lives.

• True faith involves speaking to challenges and expecting change.

• Faith works through actions, exemplified by biblical figures like Abraham and Paul.

Key Themes

- **Active Expression of Faith:** Faith must be actively expressed and voiced; it is not a silent hope but a vocal declaration that brings God's promises into reality.
- **Faith as a Foundation for Miracles:** The miraculous occurs not by chance but as a direct result of the believers' faith, positioning them as conduits for God's supernatural interventions.

- **Overcoming Doubt with Faith:** Doubt and fear are constant challenges to faith; overcoming them involves a conscious decision to trust God's word over our circumstances.
- **The Role of Faith in Daily Challenges:** Daily challenges and life's pressures test our faith, but maintaining a focus on God's truth helps us overcome and transform tough situations into testimonies.
- **Faith's Power to Alter Reality:** Faith is not passive; it is a transformative force that changes not only spiritual but physical realities, moving mountains and altering life courses.

Conclusion

"Living By Faith" underscores that faith is an active, dynamic force that shapes every aspect of the believer's life. By embracing and acting on faith, individuals can transform their realities, overcome obstacles, and fulfill their God-given destinies. Through biblical examples and practical applications, the chapter calls readers to a life where faith leads to divine encounters and miraculous transformations.

CHAPTER 39

GRIT!

Bible Verse

Luke 18:1-8 - Jesus used a parable about a persistent widow to illustrate the importance of continuous faith and prayer, demonstrating the essence of grit.

Introduction

This chapter explores the concept of grit, defined as the intersection of courage and perseverance, and its vital role in overcoming life's challenges. It draws inspiration from Theodore Roosevelt's "The Man in the Arena" speech, highlighting the value of persistence in the face of adversity.

Word of Wisdom

"Grit is conceived on the battlefield, birthed in the fire of affliction, and raised in the palace of perseverance." Kris Vallotton

Main Theme

The chapter asserts that grit is an essential quality that enables individuals to endure difficulties with determination and resilience, turning challenges into opportunities for growth.

Key Points

• Grit is uncovered through life's trials, not by comfort or ease.

• It involves staying the course even when the excitement has faded.

• True grit is often perceived as foolish by those who easily give up.

• Developing grit requires a vision that gives pain a purpose.

• Grit is about finishing what you started, regardless of the obstacles.

Key Themes

- **The Nature of Grit:** Grit transcends natural talent and is characterized by a steadfast refusal to give up in the face of trials, embodying a spirit that is essential for enduring life's toughest challenges.
- **Developing Grit:** One cultivates grit by surrounding themselves with courageous individuals, maintaining a hopeful outlook despite setbacks, and keeping focused on past victories to fuel future endeavors.

- **The Role of Vision in Sustaining Grit:** A clear vision provides direction and meaning, turning painful experiences into focused efforts toward achieving significant goals.
- **Impact of Grit on Spiritual Warfare:** Grit empowers believers to withstand spiritual assaults, as it involves unwavering faith and perseverance that can exhaust and overcome adversarial forces.
- **Practical Steps to Enhance Grit:** Engaging with like-minded, resilient individuals, setting protective goals, and embracing hopeful persistence are practical ways to develop and strengthen grit.

Conclusion

"Grit!" challenges readers to embrace their inner strength and push through the inevitable difficulties of life. By fostering grit, one can ensure they not only survive the trials but emerge victorious, having grown in character and faith. The chapter encourages readers to act on their beliefs and persistently pursue their divine calling, thereby transforming their challenges into triumphs.

CHAPTER 40

DELIVER US FROM EVIL

Bible Verse

Matthew 6:9-13 - The Lord's Prayer, a model given by Jesus, emphasizes seeking deliverance from evil as a key component of our daily petitions to God.

Introduction

This chapter delves into the profound simplicity of the Lord's Prayer, focusing on the petition to "deliver us from evil," highlighting its importance in the believer's life for maintaining spiritual health and protection.

Word of Wisdom

"Whenever I am feeling weak, depressed, or anxious, I always remind myself that Jesus is with me and that He is the one who will deliver me." Kris Vallotton

Main Theme

The chapter underscores the reliance on God's power for deliverance from evil, reinforcing the believer's need for divine intervention in daily challenges and spiritual warfare.

Key Points

• The Lord's Prayer is a foundational Christian prayer emphasizing reliance on God.

• It includes a plea for daily sustenance and deliverance from evil.

• Faith in God's deliverance is crucial in overcoming life's trials.

• Jesus provides a model of trust and dependency on God's protection.

• The importance of forgiveness and resisting temptation is highlighted.

Key Themes

- **Understanding Deliverance:**
  Deliverance from evil is not just about avoiding harm but actively engaging in spiritual warfare with the confidence that God is our protector and has the ultimate authority over all evil.
- **The Role of Faith in Deliverance:**
  Faith plays a crucial role in how we experience God's deliverance; it requires believing in God's omnipotence and His

willingness to act on behalf of His children.

- **Practical Dependence on God:** Integrating the Lord's Prayer into daily life fosters a continual dependence on God's guidance and protection, reminding us of His closeness and sovereignty.
- **Spiritual Vigilance:** Believers are encouraged to be vigilant against the forces of evil by embodying the principles taught in the Lord's Prayer, such as forgiveness and seeking God's kingdom.
- **Divine Assurance:** The promises of God as depicted in Jude 24-25 provide believers with the assurance of God's ability to keep them from falling and to present them blameless, reinforcing the power of God's deliverance.

Conclusion

"Deliver Us from Evil" calls on believers to not only recite the Lord's Prayer but to live out its profound truths. It emphasizes the necessity of divine help in overcoming evil and the power of faith to activate God's protection and guidance. The chapter encourages believers to maintain a life of prayer, vigilance, and complete reliance on God to navigate through life's challenges.

www.ingramcontent.com/pod-product-compliance
Lightning Source LLC
Chambersburg PA
CBHW071330150726
47997CB00002B/666